ON EARTH
AS IT IS IN HEAVEN

The Lord's Prayer in Forty Languages

Compiled by
Emily Gwathmey and Suzanne Slesin
Design by Stafford Cliff

Photography by
Kulbir Thandi

VIKING
STUDIO
BOOKS

VIKING STUDIO BOOKS
Published by the Penguin Group
Penguin Books USA Inc., 375 Hudson
Street, New York, New York 10014, U.S.A.
Penguin Books Ltd, 27 Wrights Lane,
London W8 5TZ England.
Penguin Books Australia Ltd,
Ringwood,Victoria, Australia.
Penguin Books Canada Ltd, 10 Alcorn
Avenue, Toronto, Ontario, Canada M4V 3B2
Penguin Books (N.Z.) Ltd, 182 -190 Wairau
Road, Auckland 10, New Zealand.

Penguin Books Ltd, Registered Offices:
Harmondsworth, Middlesex, England.

First published in 1994 by Viking Penguin,
a division of Penguin Books U.S.A. Inc.

10 9 8 7 6 5 4 3 2 1

ISBN 0-670-85011-X   CIP data available.

Printed in Singapore.

ACKNOWLEDGMENTS
We are grateful to the following people for
their support and help with this book:

Marion Adler, Faith Coleman, Mary Curtis,
Martin Durrant at the Victoria & Albert
Museum in London, Kim Edwards, Charles
S. Hirsch, Maurice Krasnow, Anne Lipow,
Patricta Proscino at the Balch Institute
library in Philadelphia, Anne J. Scher at the
Jewish Museum in New York, Sheila
Schwartz, Wendy Sclight, Jonathan Scott,
Michael Steinberg, Barbara Strauch, Ellen
Stern, and Kulbir Thandi.

Special thanks to Alex McLean for
photographing the original 1869 edition of
the Album of Language; Matt Sarraf for the
production artwork; Melvyn Alan at the
Brightside Partnership; and Philip Hughes at
the Lacquer Chest in London.

Thank you also to our agents, Lucy Kroll and
Barbara Hogenson at the Lucy Kroll Agency;
and to Michael Fragnito, Barbara Williams,
and Roni Axelrod at Viking Studio Books.

CONTENTS

DO UNTO OTHERS AS YOU WOULD HAVE THEM DO UNTO YOU

ENGLISH

ARYAN FAMILY—CLASS TEUTONIC.

UR Father which art in heaven, Hallowed be thy name. Thy kingdom come. Thy will be done in earth, as it is in heaven. Give us this day our daily bread. And forgive us our debts, as we forgive our debtors. And lead us not into temptation, but deliver us from evil: For thine is the kingdom, and the power, and the glory, for ever.

AMEN.

INTRODUCTION

THE LORD'S PRAYER is among the most ancient and powerful poems in history. Murmured in church services, at weddings and funerals, spoken by non-religious people at athletic events, and recited at the close of twelve-step meetings such as Alcoholics Anonymous and Al-Anon, the Lord's Prayer

women, reflecting their common human heritage. For nearly 2,000 years, millions have prayed and meditated upon the "Our Father," as the prayer is also known. Both the New Testament Gospels of Matthew 6: 9-13 and Luke 11: 2-4 tell us that the Lord's Prayer was first spoken by Jesus, in his native Semitic tongue of Aramaic, to his disciples during the Sermon on the Mount, in response to their request, "teach us to pray."

The ten simple lines of the prayer, to which some churches later added the ceremonial ending or amen, "for Thine is the kingdom and the power and the glory, forever," have become a common denominator of all Christian theologies. The first line is a variation on the theme of the Hebrew Kaddish, the solemn prayer recited by mourners after the death of a close relative, from Daniel 2: 20 in the Old Testament. And the words of the closing appear in the Old Testament in I Chronicles 29:11, as King David bids farewell to his people and bequeaths his throne and kingdom to Solomon, his son and heir. The holy lines of the Lord's Prayer are considered to be both an abridgment of and a model for all worship. The third-century theologian Tertullian wrote that the prayer is a summation of the Gospel (*breviarium totius evangelii*), covering all earthly and spiritual needs and all heavenly aspirations.

In today's chaotic, frightening, and isolating world, the search for spirituality and serenity has become both a personal and a communal quest. And the Lord's Prayer has become its basic text, a seemingly universal expression of faith, not only for those with a religious bent but for millions of others searching for a Higher Power of their own choosing. The words are well known and oft-quoted in all the languages of the world.

has become a universal symbol of closeness and connection. A powerful expression of spiritual unity, the prayer brings together people of widely differing faiths and beliefs who often recite the lines holding hands. Even those who are unfamiliar with its exact words allow the prayer's rhythmic phrases to act as a bond linking them to fellow men and

The prayer is also called the Paternoster, Latin for "Our Father." The use of "Our" rather than "My" father reflects the teachings of Jesus and other leaders that we are all brothers and sisters in the family of man. In *The Lord's Prayer: An Interpretation* (Harper Collins Publishers,1989), the philosopher and scientist Emmet Fox notes that Supreme Court Justice Oliver Wendell Holmes Jr. said, "My religion is summed up in the first two words of the Lord's Prayer."

Language and religion have always been inextricably entwined. In *The Story of Language* (J.B. Lippincott & Company,1965), Mario Pei writes: "Christianity found two thoroughly established languages, Latin and Greek, ready to act as its instruments, and it was thanks to Christianity that these two languages survived and spread instead of being submerged by the incoming waves of foreign-speaking barbarians. Adoption of the religion carried with it adoption of the language indissolubly bound with that religion." Over the centuries, as Christianity reached further afield, the Bible was translated into the modern tongues spoken by different peoples around the world.

This sense of being a link in a universal and wide-reaching chain stretching back to antiquity elicited a responsive chord in us when we first discovered *The Album of Language, Illustrated by the Lord's Prayer in One Hundred Languages* about two years ago. The large and hefty tome, with an embossed tan cover and intricately decorated pages, was originally published in 1869 by J. B. Lippincott & Company of Philadelphia. Compiled by G. Naphegyi, the book offered "historical descriptions of the principal languages, interlinear translations and pronunciation of each prayer, a dissertation on the languages of the world, and tables exhibiting all known languages, dead and living." This *Album of Language* was not a unique work. Rather, it was one of many similar volumes produced in the second part

of the nineteenth century, including a turn-of-the-century English version featuring the Lord's Prayer in 500 languages. Elaborately hand-crafted and over-sized polyglot Bibles were also a convention of that era. Accessible and portable, these books served the needs of the numerous Christian missionaries, who were following the New Testament injunction, "Go ye into all the world and preach the Gospel to every creature."

LATIN

ARYAN FAMILY, NORTHERN DIVISION.
DEAD LANGUAGE. LATIN. LINGUA VULGARIS. CLASS, ITALIC.
VULGATE, PARIS, 1793.

PATER NOSTER

qui es in cœlis:
Sanctificetur nomen tuum.
Adveniat regnum tuum.
Fiat voluntas tua,
sicut in cœlo, et in terra.
Panem nostrum supersubstantialem [quotidianum]
da nobis hodie.
Et dimitte [remitte] nobis debita nostra, sicut et
nos dimittimus debitoribus nostris.
Et ne nos inducas in tentationem, sed libera nos
a malo [ab illo malo].
Nam [quia] tuum est regnum, et imperium
[potentia], et magnificentia
[gloria], in sempiterno [secula seculorum].

AMEN

With the Lord's Prayer as its common denominator, the languages represented in the 1869 *Album* range from ancient to modern. Included are the expected Spanish, Italian, French, German, and Greek; the more unusual Cherokee, Javanese, Welsh, and Bengal, and a few more arcane dialects like Samaritan, Sanskrit, and Hottentot, all organized into six linguistic families: Aryan,

Semitic, Turanian, Oceanic, African, and American. Based on the King James version of the Bible, the text uses the words "debt" and "debtors" in the sixth petition, as transcribed in the Book of Matthew. By contrast, the Protestant and Episcopal Churches chose to employ the words "trespasses" and "trespass" in their recitation of the prayer, based on the transcription found in the Gospel According to St. Luke.

Although uncomfortable with the book's original missionary purpose of conquest and conversion, we felt that there was something particularly compelling for our times in the large number of possible expressions of the Lord's Prayer. In the same way that the prayer is comforting, inclusionary, and generous in its tenets, so, it seemed, was its deployment in the myriad languages of the world. Turning the thick, yellowed pages of the book, we found ourselves mesmerized as much by the transliteration into familiar languages as by the visual appearance of the more exotic and mysterious tongues.

We chose to re-interpret the original by distilling it into forty languages, a number significant in Biblical and mystical lore as an elevation of four, "the universal whole." Moses waited forty days and nights on Mt. Sinai before receiving the tablets of law. The Israelites wandered for forty years in the desert. Lent signifies Jesus' forty-day fast in the wilderness. The Koran should be read every forty days. A period of sanctuary or privilege constitutes forty days' grace.

For our book, we chose both the familiar, still-spoken tongues from the original as well as some of the more esoteric. Ancient Latin seemed important to include, as did Greek, the language into which the prayer was originally translated from Aramaic. (Because of this, reciting the prayer in Greek is widely believed to be supremely holy.) We have not altered the translations

from the original volume, but have reproduced them with all their inexactitudes.

Commenting on the Lord's Prayer, Simone Weil, the modern French philosopher and mystic, has written: "The 'Our Father' contains all possible petitions; we cannot conceive of any prayer not already contained in it. It is to prayer what Christ is to humanity. It is impossible to say it once through, giving the fullest possible attention to each word, without

a change, infinitesimal perhaps but real, taking place in the soul."

We hope that by reading the Lord's Prayer, in one or many languages, either in recognition or rediscovery, you will be drawn to its timeless power as we were and continue to be.

SPANISH

ARYAN FAMILY, NORTHERN DIVISION.
DEAD LANGUAGE, LANGUE D'OC.—OSCAN. CLASS, ITALIC.
P. SCIO MIGUEL, LONDON, 1819.

PADRE NUESTRO, QUE ÉSTAS EN LOS CIELOS; SANCTIFICADO SEA ÉL TU NOMBRE. VENGA ÉL TU REYNO. HÁGASE TU VOLUNTAD, COMO EN EL CIELO, ASÍ TAMBIEN EN LA TIERRA. DANOS HOY NUESTRO PAN SOBRE SUBSTANCIAL [COTIDIANO].

Y PERDÓNANOS NUESTRAS DEUDAS ASÍ COMO NOSOTROS PERDONAMOS Á NUESTROS DEUDORES. Y NO NOS DEJES CAER EN TENTACION, MAS LIBRANOS DE MAL. PORQUE TUYO ES EL REYNO, EL PODER Y LA GLORIA POR LOS SIGLOS.

Amen.

BRAZILIAN

OR

GUARANIC

SOUTH AMERICAN LANGUAGE.

RERÚBA, IBÁPE EREÍBAE, IMBOYERO-
BIÂ RIPIRAMÔ NDERÉRA TOYCO. TOUN-
DERECOMÁVÂN GATÚORÉBE. NDERE-
MIMBOTÁRA TIYAYE IBIPE IBAPE YYÂ-
YÊYÂBÉ. OREREMBIU ARA NÂBÔGUÂRA
EMÊÉ COÁRA PIPEORÊBE. NDENYRÔ
OREYNÁNGAI PÁBAEUPE ORÉBE MÁRÁHÁRUPÊ ORE-
NYR ÔNÚNGÁ HAEOREPO EYÂRIMÉ. TOREMBOÁ IMÉ-
GAN OAIPÁ; OREPICYRO EPECATU MBAE POCHI GUÎ.

Amen

CATALONIAN.

Pare nostro, que estau en lo Cel,
Father our, who art in the heaven,

Sanctificat sea el vostre sant Nom;
hallowed be the your holy name;

Vinga en nos altres el vostré sant Reine;
come to us us the your holy kingdom;

Fasas la vostra Voluntat, axi en la Terra, coma se
be done the your will, as in the earth, so be

fa en lo Cel;
done in the heaven;

El Pa nostre de cada Dia da nous lo gui;
the bread ours of each day give us the day;

I perdonau nos nostres Culpes, axi com nos altres
and forgive us our faults, as also we we

perdonam a nostres Deudores;
forgive to our debtors;

I no permetau, que nos altres caigam en la
and not permit that we fall in the

Tentacio;
temptation;

Ans desllibra nos de qualsevol Mal.
but deliver us from whatever evil.

Amen.
Amen.

To ....

From ....

19

16

17

11

14

31

30

28

ON EARTH
AS IT IS IN HEAVEN

Suffer the little children to come unto me.—Mark 10: 14.
I will gather all nations and tongues.—Isa. 66: 18.

The Album of Language illustrated by the

Lord's Prayer in One hundred Languages.

BY G. NAPHEGYI, M.D., A.M.

Member of the "Sociedad Geografica y Estadistica" of Mexico,
and "Mejoras Materiales" of Texoco.

Lith.& Printed in colors
630 Chestnut St.

Published
BY
J.B. LIPPINCOTT
& Co.

by Edward Herline,
Philadelphia.

PHILADELPHIA.

PORTUGUESE

ARYAN FAMILY, NORTHERN DIVISION.
CLASS, ITALIC.

PAI NOSSO, QUEM ESTAS NOS CEOS,
SANCTIFICADO SEJA TEU NOME.
VENHA TEU REYNO. SEJA FEITA
TUA VONTADE ASSI NA TERRA, COMO NOS
CEOS. O PAO NOSSO DE CADA DIA NOS DA HOJE.
E PERDOA NOS NOSSAS DIVIDAS, ASSI COMO NOS
PERDOAMOS A NOSSOS DEVIDORES. E NOS NAO
DES CAHIR EM TENTAÇAO; MAS LIVRA NOS DE MAL. POR-
QUE TEU HE O REYNO, E O PODER, E A GLORIA, PARA TODO
SEMPRE.

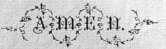

AMEN.

[Burmese script text]

BURMESE.

SOUTH ASIA. TURANIAN FAMILY.

Ō̤ kaungh-kaeng-waej né-tâu-mû-sau-kjūn-tâu-to-apha-kha-mi-
Ō̤   heaven in   being   high   who   servant   high father elevated,

tâu,

Koj-tâu-amī-nâma-tâu ro-se-mrat-nōh-si-phïīt-k'ê;
self-elevated   name   honored   keep   sending;

Koj-tâu-naing-ngan-tâu-ti-si-phïīt-k'ê;
self-elevated kingdom raised reached being sending;

Koj-tâu-alō-tâu kaungh-kaeng-nhaik pri-k'on sakaé-só pathawi-
self   will raised   heaven in carried out   being   carried out

mrê-krïh-apâu pri-k'on-sï-phrït-k'ê kjūn;
earth on   carried out   done sending;

Tau-to né-taing asaek-shaeng-lauk-ak'âh-a-hârâ ja-né k'jūn-tâu-
servant   each day   life   enough   food   this day   servant

tó-âh kaej-ma-sanâh-tâu-mû-pâ;
raised   helping merciful   raised;

Kjūn-tâu-tó-sï-lï kjūn-tâu-tó krïūêh-mrï-taeng-sau-lû-to-âh-sû-
servant raised and   servant   raised   debt   make   men   them

tó-krïūêh-mrï-taeng-sï-mha kaej-kaengh-sakáe-so kjūn-tâu-tó-
offences   to carry   forgive as   servant raised

krïūêh-mrï-phrït-sau-aprït-nga-rae-mjâh-mha-li kaej-kaengh-
debt being   which   sin   also   helping   forgiven

tâu-mû-pâ;
raised;

K'âh-k'am-khraengh-arâ-taeng-li kjūn-tâu-tó-kō ma-jû-ma-
temptation   opportunity in   and servant raised   not

k'haung-tâu-mû-ruê ma-kaung-ma-saéng-sï-amhu-arâ tó-
lead   raised and   not good   not proper   cases

mha kjūn-tâu-tó-kō kûh-mrauk-kaej-kaengh-tâu-mû-pâ;
from   servant raised   deliver and free   raised;

Asaej-kraung-nili-hû-mû-kâli koj-tâu-âh ak'ïn-ma-pïrat naing-
which through   self raised   now not ending   kingdom

ngan-tâu ak'ūm satti gon'-kjê-g'jah-tâu-phrït-k'ê-sï-tï.
raised   power   glory raised   being send.

Âmên.
Amen.

KASHMIR

TURANIAN FAMILY.
AS PRONOUNCED BY THE ENGLISH IN THE EAST INDIES.

I SWURG UNDUR ROOJUNWALI SARI MALI, TOOHUNDOO NAM PUVITRA SUMPNI. TOOHUNDOO RAJ YIYE. TOOHI KHATIR KHAHSWURGUS UNDUR YESOO DHURTEE UNDUR KURAN YIYE. USE JORUS LAYUK KHORUK USI AJ DEYIW. BHIYA SAROOROON USE MAPH KURIW, YISOO USE PUNUNIN KURUJDARUN MAPH KURAN CHHOO BHIYA USE PUREECH HAY UNDER MUH HEYIW. LEKIN BOORAEEYANISH TRUWIW; KANJI RAJ BHIYA PURAKRUM BHIYA MUHIMA HUMESH TOOHI CHHOW.

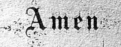

H. H. The Maharaja of Mysore.
H. H. The Maharaja Gaekwar of Baroda.   H. H. The Maharaja of Gwalior and Sindhia.
H. H. The Maharaja of Kashmir and Jammu.
H. H. The Maharaja of Travancore.   H. H. The Nawab of Bahawalpur.

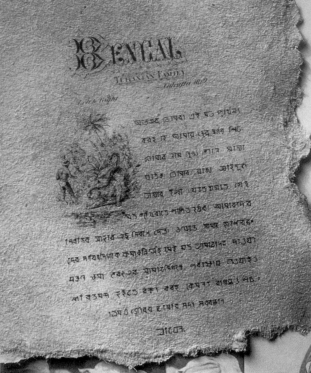

BENGALEE

ARYAN FAMILY. PORTUGUESE PRONUNCIATION.

Pita amardiguer, poromo Xorgué asso,
Father   bour   heaven

Tomar xidhi nameré xeba houcq;
thy   name

Aixuq amardiguere tomar Raizot;
                        kingdom

Tomar ze icha xei houq, zemon Porthibité, temon
                         as   earth   as

Xorgué;
heaven

Amardiguer protidiner ahar amardiguere azica dio;

amardiguer corzo ghemo, zemon amora ghemi
           debts   debts

amardiguer corziore;

Amardiguere cumotité porrité na dio;

Ar amardiguere xocol mouddo hote raquia coro.
for

Amen.
Amen

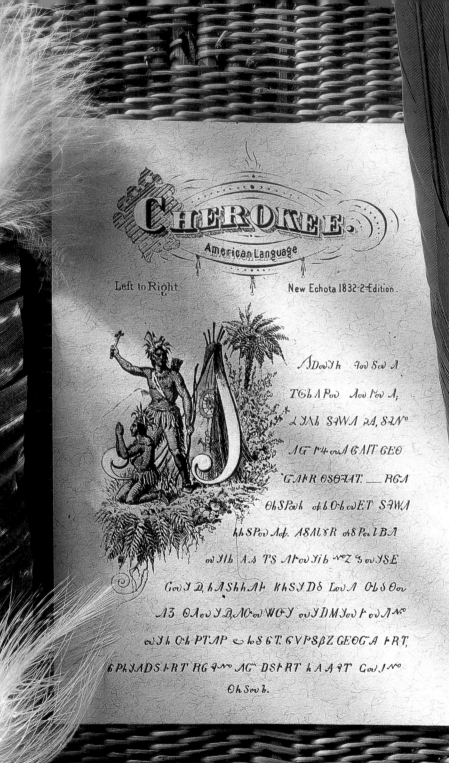

CHEROKEE.

American Language

Left to Right   New Echota 1832 2 Edition.

Modern French

Aryan Family, Northern Division.
Class, Italic.

NOTRE PÈRE, QUI ES AU CIEL, TON NOM SOIT SANCTIFIÉ. TON REGNE VIENNE. TA VOLONTÉ SOIT FAITE SUR LA TERRE, COMME AU CIEL. DONNE-NOUS AUJOURD'HUI NOTRE PAIN QUOTIDIEN. ET PARDONNE-NOUS NOS OFFENSES, COMME NOUS LES PARDONNONS À CEUX QUI NOUS ONT OFFENSÉS. ET NE NOUS INDUIS POINT EN TENTATION; MAIS DÉLIVRE NOUS DU MAL. CAR C'EST À TOI QU'APPARTIENT LE RÈGNE, LA PUISSANCE, ET LA GLOIRE.

AMEN

MIGMAG

AMERICAN LANGUAGE.

Uchiak uaiok ebin, Kehijurek kech kermurek ignemuiek. Ooiok evidadeziben ignemuiek. Chuk-
turideziben ignemuiek telamokchitich oaiok ekkik
chaktachkik.   Kichku nir unan echimuiek ndo
echimideziben markodemideziben.   Uinsoudi mu
ktigariu telamok uinsoudi dmigik ninen mu ktigariock.   Mu to
tentationka pemiedeziben ignemuiek; meruich kechinoguambit uin-
cinigil tuahtuick.

Uelek eta Jesus.

DELAWARE

NORTH AMERICAN.

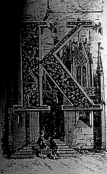KI WETOCHEMELENK, TALLI EPIAN AWOSSA-GAME. MACHELENDASUTSCH KTELLEWUN-SOWOAGAN. KSAKIMAWOAGAN PEJEWI-GETSCH. KTELITE HEWOAGAN LEGETSCH TALLI ACHQUIDHACKAMICKE, ELGIQUI LECK TALLI AWOSSAGAME. MILINEEN ELGISCH-QUIK GUNIGISCHUK ACHPOAN. WOAK MI-WELENDAMMAUWINEEN 'N TSCHANNAUCH-SOWOAGANNENA, ELGIQUI NILUNA MIWE-LENDAMMAUWENK NIK TSCHETSCHANILAWEQUENGIK, WOAK KATSCHI 'NPAWUNEEN LI ACHQUETSCHIECHTOWOAGANUNG, TSCHU-KUND KTENNICEN UNTSCHI MEDHICKUNG. ALOD KNIHILLATA-MEN KSAKIMAWOAGAN, WOAK KTALLOWILUSSOWOAGAN, NE WUNTSCHI HALLEMIWI LI HALLAMAGAMIK.

HUNGARIAN

TURANIAN FAMILY, NORTHERN DIVISION.
LANGUAGE OF THE MAYGARS. BRANCH, UGRIC. CLASS, URALIC.
FROM BARON SZEPESY'S TRANSLATION.

Mi atyánk, ki vagy mennyekben, Szenteltessék a' te neved. Jöjjön te országod. Légnen te akaratod miképen mennyben azonképen a' földön is. Mindennapi kenyerünk adjad nekünk ma. És bocsásdmeg nekünk a' mi vétkeinket, miképen mi is megbocsátunk ellenünk vétetteknek. És ne vigy minket a' késértetbe; de szabadits a' gonosztól.

HUNGARIAN.

Mi atyánk, ki vagy mennyekben,
Our Father our who , art heaven-in,

Szentellessék a' te neved;
hallowed be the thy name thine;

Jöjjön te országod;
come thou kingdom thine;

Légyen te akaratod miképen mennyben azonké-
be thy will thine as heaven in also

pen a' földön is;
the earth on also;

Mindennapi kenyerünket adjad nekünk ma;
daily bread our give us to-day;

'Es bocsásdmeg nekünk a' mi vetkeinket, miképen
and pardon us the our debt ours, as

mi is megbocsátunk ellenünk vettetteknek;
we also forgive we against us debtors;

'Es ne vigy minket a' késértetbe;
and not lead us the temptation in;

De szabadíts a' gonosztol.
but deliver the evil from.

Amen.

FINLANDISH

Turanian Family, Northern Division.
Dialect of the Finn. Branch, Chudic. Class, Finnic.
Tornea, 1815.

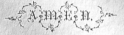

Isä meidän, joka olet taiwaisa:
Pyhitetty olkon sinun nimes. Lähestykön sinun waldakundas. Olkon sinun tahtos, niin maasa, kuin taiwasa. Anna meille tänäpänä meidän jokapäiwäinen leipämme. Ja anna meille meidän welkamme anderi, niinkuin mekin anderi annamme meidän welwollistemme. Ja älä johdata meitä kiusauxen, mutta päästä meitä pahasta. Sillä sinun on waldakunda, ja woima, ja kunnia, ijankaikkisesti.

A·M·E·N.

FINNISH.

From the "Biblia di Pyhä Raamattu:" St. Petersburg, 1817.

Jsä meidän, joka olet taiwaisa,
Father our who thou art in heaven,

Pyhitetty olkon sinun nimes;
hallowed be thy name;

Lähestykön sinun waldakundas;
come thy kingdom;

Olkon sinun tahtos, niin maasa, kuin taiwasa;
be thy will so on earth as in heaven;

Anna meille tänäpänä meidän jokapäiwäinen
give us this day our all-daily

leipämme;
bread;

Ja anna meille meidän welkamme andexi,
and give us our debt forgiveness

niinkuin mekin andexi annamme meidän
as also we forgiveness give our

welwollistemme;
debtors;

Ja älä johdata meitä kiusauxeen;
and not lead us in temptation;

Mutta päästä meitä pahasta:
but deliver us from evil:

Sillä sinun on waldakunda, ja woima, ja kunnia,
for thine is the kingdom and power and honor

ijankaikkisesti.
in eternity. Amen.

DANISH

ARYAN FAMILY, NORTHERN DIVISION.
DEAD LANGUAGE, OLD NORSE. BRANCH, SCANDINAVIAN. CLASS, TEUTONIC.
COPENHAGEN, 1819.

Vor Fader, du som er i himlene: helliget vorde dit navn. Komme dit rige; skee din villie, som i himmelen, saa og paa yorden. Giv os i dag vort daglige bröd. Og forlad os vor skyld, saa som vi og forlade vore skyldener. Og leed os ikke ind i fristelse: men frie os fra det onde. Thi dit er riget, og kraften, og herligheden, i evighed.

Amen.

DANISH.

From "Nye Testamente:" London, 1814.

Vor Fader, du som er i himlene,
Our Father thou art is in heaven,

Helliget vorde dit navn;
hallowed be thy name;

Komme dit rige;
come thy kingdom;

Skee din villie, som i himmelen, saa og paa yorden;
done be thy will, heaven, as (also) and on earth;

Giv os i dag vort daglige bröd;
give us the day our daily bread;

Og forlad os vor skyld, saa vi og forlade vore
and forgive us our debts as we and forgive our

skyldener;
debtors;

Og leed os ikke ind i fristelse;
and lead us not in the temptation;

Men frie os fra det onde;
but free us from the evil;

Thi dit er riget, og kraften, og herligheden i
for thine the kingdom, and power, and glory in

evighed.
eternity.

Amen.
Amen.

The Finnish Workers' Band

Warren Ohio — 1920

NORWEGIAN

ARYAN FAMILY, NORTHERN DIVISION.
CLASS, SCANDINAVIAN.

Vor Fader, du som est y Himmelen, Gehailiget worde dit
Nafu. Tilkomma os Riga
dit. Din Wilia geskia paa Jorden, som
haudt er udi Himmelen. Giff os y Tag
wort dagliga Brouta. Och forlaet os
wort Skioldt, som wy forlata wora
Skioldouar. Och lad os ickie komma udi Fristelse; man frals os fra Onet. Thy Rigit er dit,
Macht och Kracht, fra Evighait til Evighait.
Amen.

NORWEGIAN.

ORKNEYS DIALECT.

Fauor i ir i Chimrie,
Helleur ir i Nam thite;
Gilla Cofdum thite cumma;
Veya thine mota vara gort o Yurn, sinna gort i
    Chimrie;
Gav us da on da dalight Brow vora;
Firgive uus Sinna uora sin vee firgive Sindara
    mutha uus;
Lyv uus ye i Tumtation;
Min delivera uus fro olt Ilt.
Amen, on sa meteth vera.

SWEDISH

ARYAN FAMILY, NORTHERN DIVISION.
DEAD LANGUAGE, OLD NORSE. BRANCH, SCANDINAVIAN. CLASS, TEUTONIC.
FROM "NEGA TESTAMENTET," STOCKHOLM, 1824.

 ader wår, som äst i himlom; Helgadt warde ditt namn. Tillkomme ditt rike. Ske din wilye, såsom i himmelen, så ock på yorden. Wårt dageliga bröd gif oss i dag. Och förlåt oss våra skulder, såsom och vi förlåte dem oss skyldige äro. Och inled oss icke i frestelse; utan fräls oss ifrån ondo. Ty riket är ditt, och magten, och härligheten i ewighet.

Amen

SWEDISH.

From "Nya Testamentet," Stockholm, 1824.

Fader wår, som ast i himlom,
Father our, who art in heaven,

Helgadt warde ditt namn;
hallowed be thy name;

Tillkomme ditt rike;
it come thy kingdom;

Ske din wilye, såsom i himmelen, så ock på yorden;
be done thine will, as is in heaven, as also on earth;

Wårt dageliga bröd gif oss i dag;
our daily bread give us the day;

Och förlåt oss våra skulder, såsom och vi förlåte
and forgive us our debts, as also we forgive

dem oss skyldige äro;
those our debtors;

Och inled oss icke i frestelse;
and lead us not the temptation;

Utan fräls oss ifrån ondo:
but free us from evil:

Ty riket är ditt, och magten, och härligheten i
the kingdom is thine and power, and glory in

ewighet.
eternity.

Amen.
Amen.

GIPSY

ARYAN FAMILY. CLASS, INDIC.

maro Dada, ote andre o Tarpe, macharificable sinele tun nao. Abillele tun chim. Sinele querdi tun pesquital andre a jolile, sasta andre o Tarpe. Dinnananque achibes amaro manro de cada chibis. Y amangue ertina amarias visabas, andiar sasta muertinamos a os sares, sos debisarelen amangue buchi. Y na enseeles amangue andre o chungalo y choro.

Amin.

GIPSY.

ARYAN FAMILY. CLASS, INDIC.

Amaro Dada, oté andre o Tarpe,
Our Father there in the heaven,

Macharificable sinele tun naó.
hallowed be thy name.

Abillele tun chim.
come thy kingdom.

Sinele querdi tun pesquital andré a jolile, sasta
be done thy will on the earth, as also

andré o Tarpe.
in the heaven.

Dinnananque achibes amaro manro de cada chibis.
give us to-day our bread of every day,

Y amangue ertina amarias visabas,
and us pardon our debts,

Andiar sasta muertinamos á os sares, sos
as we also we forgive to all those who

debisarelen amangue buchi.
sin against us something.

Y na enseeles amangue andre o chungalo y choro.
and not lead us in the temptation and evil.

Amin.
Amen.

TURKISH

Semitic Family Class Arabic

Constantinople 1814.

أصلك خان قلوب و چله دك
اى كوكلو و على ابامز
أملك مقدر اولسون
ملكوت لاسون كوكده مد
اللّه لعه اسه بزرسى دیله
اولسون جن كو نكانتا
حر كو لو دكو نووز * ونز هو جلم مرى باعشله
نحن بزدی لاعنو چلرلر لاننده ننقال رز
مبك اعواها عله الأی حسدف قور
قر جن عيلک و قوّة و عزّه اّنا سنكدد
امين

TURKISH.

Bisum Baba-müs ki Kjokler-deh sin,
Our   Father   our   who   heaven   in   art,

Senüng Ad-üng mukaddes olsun;
thine (tui) name thine (tua)   hallowed   be;

Senüng Meleut-üng kielsun;
thine (tui)   kingdom thine (tuum)   come;

Senüng Iradet-üng olsun nitekim (also, betschahke)
thine (tui)   will thine (tuum) be   as also   (as also)

Kjok-deh dachi Jer-deh;
heaven in   also   earth in;

Her kjunki bisüm Etmeke-müsi wer bise bu Kjun;
every daily   our   bread   our   give us   this day;

We-bisüm Burdschler-ümi bise baggischleh,
and our   debts ours   us   forgive,

nitekim (also, betschahke) bis dachi bisüm
as also   (as also)   we   also   ours

Burdschlüler-ümüsi baggischlerus;
debtors   ours   we forgive;

We-bisi Tadschribe adehal etma;
and us (nos) in temptation   entry   make not;

Lekin Scherir-den bisi Nedschat ejle;
but   evil from us   delivery   make;

Sira senüng-dür Meleut, we-Sultanet, we-Medschdi,
for thine (tui) is   kingdom, and   power,   and   praise,

ta Ebbed.
to eternity.

Amin.
Amen.

WELSH.

ARYAN FAMILY, NORTHERN DIVISION.

DEAD LANGUAGE. CORNISH. BRANCH, CYMRIC. CLASS, CELTIC.

OMBRIC, LONDON, 1831.

EIN TAD, yr hwn, wyt yn y nefoedd, sancteiddier dy Enw. Deled dy deyrnas. Gwneler dy ewyllys, megis yn ynef, felly ar y ddaear hefyd. Dym i ni heddyw ein bara beunyddiol. A maddeu i ni ein dyledion fel y maddeuwn ninnau i'n dyledwyr. Ac nac arwain ni i brofedigaeth, eithr gwared ni rhag drwg. Canyseiddot ti yw y deyrnas, a'r nerth a'r gogoniant yn oes oesoedd.

AMEN

Bridge

Wadi

Spring

HAIFA

HEBREW.

SEMITIC FAMILY. DIALECT OF THE JEWS. CLASS, HEBRAIC.

Abi-nu she-ba-sho-ma-yim,
Father our who in the heaven;

Yik-ka-desh she-me-cho,
hallowed be name thine,

To-ba mal-chut-cho,
come kingdom thine,

Ye-hi Rezon-echo ka-asher ba-sho,ma-yim we-ken
It be will thine as in heaven also

ba arez.
on earth.

La,cham chu-ke-nu ten lo-nu ha-yom,
Bread needful give us to-day,

Us-lach lanu eth Choboth-enu, ka-a-sher anachnu
And forgive us the sin our, as likewise we

so-le-chim le-Baale Choboth-enu.
forgive to those who sin us.

We-al thebi-enu le-Naso,
and not lead us in temptation,

Ki-im hazzil-enu min ho-ro-o.
but also deliver us from evil.

Ki l'-echo ha-mam-lo-cho, w-Hag-vu-roh
for thine the kingdom and power

w-ha-tif-eres-le Olam Olamim.
and glory from the eternity to eternity.

Omen.
Amen.'

CHINESE
Mandarin Dialect.
TURANIAN FAMILY.

Morrison & Milne Canton 1823. From the Right & from the Top down.

故此而如此所禧
等苦也云我等父在天者
放我等負債如我等赦負債我
如於天焉賜我等以日用糧
至而旨成行於地
而名成聖而王就
苦權苦榮苦於世世
敌我等出凶惡蓋而爲之國
等苦也勿由我等入誘惑乃
亞吶

CHINESE.

From Adelung's Mithridates.

TSCHU, KYNG
LORD, PRAYER.

Tsai tien tsche ngo teng fu ngo teng yuen ul ming
(art in) (heaven) (who) (our) (Father) (we) (pray) (thy) (name)

kien shing ul kue lin ke ul tshing hing yü
(be hallowed) (thy) (kingdom) (come) (near) (thy) (will) (be carried out) (in)

ty ju yü tien yen ngo teng yang ul kin je
(earth) (is) (in) (heaven) (and) (we) (hope) (thou) (in) (to-day)

yü ngo ngo je yum liang ul mien ngo tchay ju
(give) (us) (our) (daily) (food) (thou) (forgive) (our) (debt) (as)

ye mien fu ngo chay tche yeu pu ngo hiü
(also) (forgive) (our) (debt) (which) (also) (not) (us) (let)

hien yu yai kan nai kieu ngo yü hitieg ya men
(fall in) (temptation) (but) (save) (us) (from) (evil) (A-men)

WELSH.

ARYAN FAMILY, NORTHERN DIVISION. BRANCH, CYMRIC. CLASS, CELTIC.

Ein Tad, yr hwn wyt yn y nefoedd,
Our Father, who art in the heaven,

Sancteiddier dy Enw;
hallowed be thy name;

Deled dy deyrnas;
it come thy kingdom;

Gwneler dy ewyllys, megis yn y nef, felly ar y
be done thy will, as in the heaven, so on the

ddaear hefyd;
earth also;

Dyro i ni heddyw ein bara beunyddiol;
give us to-day our bread daily;

A maddeu i ni ein dyledion, fel y maddeuwn
and forgive us our debts, as forgive

ninnau i'n dyledwyr;
we our debtors;

Ac nac arwain ni i brofedigaeth;
and not lead us in temptation;

Eithr gwared ni rhag drwg:
but deliver us from evil:

Canys eiddot ti yw y deyrnas, a'r nerth, a'r
for thine is the kingdom, and the power, and

gogoniant, yn oes oesoedd.
the glory, in eternity to eternity.

Amen.
Amen.

CONFUCIUS

SUN YAT SEN

CHINA

GERMAN.

Aryan Family, Northern Division.
Dead Language. Middle High-German. Branch, High-German. Class, Teutonic.
Leander van Ness, Sulzbach, 1846.

Unſer Vater,
der du im Himmel biſt! Geheiliget werde dein Name! Dein Reich kom-me! Dein Wille geſchehe wie im Himmel alſo auch auf Erden! Gieb uns heute unſer tägliches Brod! Und vergieb uns unſere Schulden, wie auch wir vergeben unſern Schuldigern. Und führe uns nicht in Verſuchung, ſondern erlöſe uns vom Uebel, denn dein iſt das Reich, und die Kraft, und die Herrlichkeit, in Ewigkeit.

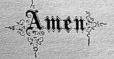

Amen

پس برین طریق دعا نما

تک شمایله: ای پدر مایه در

آسمانستای نلم تو مقدّ

س باد در صلکوت تو بیا

باد آن ان جهان که در

آسمان است بد زمین

ازالت تو نافذبار نار روزیه

مارا در این روز با بحش: دان چنا د

ترضلاران جرداری بخشیم ترن ناى

بار احما بخش ومارا در ترض آزمایش میار

بلکه از شر م خلاصی که زیرله ملک د

تو رت وجلال تا ابد ازان تر است

آمن

PERSIAN.

ARYAN FAMILY. CLASS, IRANIC.

Ei bashende-i âsumân pederi mâ,
<small>being in heaven Father our,</small>

Nami tu pak bad;
<small>name thy hallowed be;</small>

Padishahi-i tu bijajed;
<small>kingdom thy come;</small>

Meshijjeti tu tshunântshi der asuman est der
<small>will thy as also in heaven is on</small>

dunja kerde;
<small>earth be done;</small>

Shuwed sezâwâri zindegani-i ma chorâki ma
<small>it be needed that to live our bread our</small>

imruz bema bidih;
<small>to-day us give;</small>

We karzi mârâ bemâ mu-âf kun tshunântshi ma
<small>and debt ours us pardon also as we</small>

karzdarani chodrâ mu-âf mikunim;
<small>our debtors ours forgive making;</small>

We mara der azmaish mejendaz;
<small>and us in temptation not lead;</small>

Belki ez bedi nedjat bidih tshirâki;
<small>but from evil delivery give but;</small>

Padishâhi we kudret u djelâl hemishe turast.
<small>the kingdom and the power and glory always is thine.</small>

Отче нашъ, сущїй на небесахъ! да свѧтится имѧ Твое; Да прїидетъ царствїе Твое, да будетъ волѧ Твоѧ, и на земли, какъ на небеси, Хлѣбъ нашъ насущный дай намъ на сей день, И прости намъ долги наши, какъ и мы прощаемъ должникамъ нашимъ, И не предай насъ искушенїю, но избавь насъ отъ лукаваго, Ибо Твое есть царство, и сила, и слава во вѣки,

Аминь.

HOTTENTOT

TURANIAN FAMILY.
SOUTH AFRICA.

CITA BÓ, T? HOMME INGÁ T' SIHA, T?
SA DI KAMINK OUNA. HEM KOU-
QUEENT SEE. DANI HINQUA T' SA
INHEE K? CHOU KI QUIQUO T? HOMM'
INGA. MAA CITA HECI CITA KÓUA
SÉQUA BREE. K? HOM CITA CITA
HIAHINGHEE QUIQUO CITA K? HOM
CITA DÓUA KÓUNA. TIRE CITA K? CHÓÁ T? AU-
THUMMÁ, K' HAMTA CITA HI AQUEI HEE K' DOU
AUNA. T? AATS KOUQUEETSA, HIQUE T? AATS
DIAHA, HIQUE OCCISA HA, NAUWI.

RUSSIAN.

After Emperor Alexander's Order of 1823. New Translation of the Bible.

Ottshe nash, sushtshij na nebesach,
Father   our   being   in   heaven,

Da svjatitsä imjä twoye;
that   holy is   name   thine;

Da priidet carstwije twoye;
that   come   kingdom   thine;

Da budet wolja twoya i na zemlje kak na nebje;
that   be   will   thine also on   earth   as   in   heaven;

Chljeb nash nasushtshnyj daj nam na sej denj;
bread   ours   necessarily   give   us   on this   day;

I prostji nam dolgi nashi, kak i my proshtshajem
and forgive   us   debts   our   as also we   forgive

    dolxnikam nashim;
    debtors   ours;

I ne predaj nas iskusheniju;
and not deliver over   us   temptation;

No izbawj nas ot lukawago:
but   deliver   us from   evil:

Ibo twoye jestyi carstwo i sila i slava wo wyeki.
for   thine   is   kingdom and power and glory   in   eternity.

Aminj.
Amen.

Vol. 3. p. 13

The Apparel of the Hottentot//

HOTTENTOT.

SOUTH AFRICA. TURANIAN FAMILY.

Cita bô, t? homme ingá t' siha,
Our Father, who thou praised art;

T? sa di kanìnk ouna;
hallowed be thy name;

Hem kouqueent see;
thine Lordship come;

Dani ninqua t' sa inhee k? chou ki quiquo t?
thy will be done on the earth as in

homm' inga;
the heaven;

Maa cita heci cita kôua séqua brée;
give us to-day our daily bread;

K? hom cita cita hiahinghee quiquo cita k? hom
forgive us our debt as we forgive

cita dóua kôuna;
our our debtors;

Tire cita k? chôá t? Authummá;
lead us not in bad temptation;

— K' hamta cita hi aquei hee k' dou
but deliver us from the evil man;

— T? aats kouqueetsa, hique aats diaha, hique
for thine is the kingdom, and the power, and the

oecisa ha, nauwi.
glory, in eternity.

IRISH.

ARYAN FAMILY, NORTHERN DIVISION. CLASS, CELTIC. BRANCH, GADHELIC.

From J. O'Donovan's Grammar of the Irish Language: Dublin, 1845.

A athair fil hi nimib,
O Father who art in heaven,

Noemthar thainm;
hallowed be thy name;

Tod do flaithius;
it come thy kingdom;

Did do toil i talmain amail atà in nim;
it be thy will on earth as which in heaven;

Tabair dun indiu ar sasad lathi,
give us this day our daily bread,

Ocus log dun ar fiachu amail logmaitne diar
and forgive us our trespasses, as we forgive our

fhechemnaib;
debtors;

Ocus nis lecca sind i n-amus n-dofulachtai,
and not let fall us in unsupportable temptation,

Acht ron soer o cech ulc.
but deliver us from each evil.

Amen rofir.
Amen, be it true.

MAYU, OR YUCATEKIC.

Cayum ianech ti càannob,
Our Father who thou art in   heaven,

Cilichthantabac akaba;
hallowed be   thy name;

Tac a ahaulil c' okol;
it come thy kingdom   us   over;

Mencahac a uolah uai ti luum bai ti caane;
done be   thy   will   as on earth   as in heaven;

Zanzamal uah ca azotoon helelae;
daily   bread us   give   today;

Caazaatez c' ziipil he bik c' zaatzic uziipil
us forgive   our   sin   as   we   forgive   their sins

ahziipiloobtoone;
to sinners;

Ma ix appatic c' lubul ti tuntah;
nor also   let   us   fall in temptation;

Caatocoon ti lob.
us deliver   from evil.

MAYU

YUCATEKIC

*AYUM ianech ti càannob, Cilich-
thantabac akaba. Tac a ahaulil
c' okol. Mencahac a uolah uai
ti luum bai ti caane. Zanzamal
uah ca azotoon helelae. Caazaatez c' ziipil he
bik c' zaatzic uziipil ahziipiloobtoone. Ma ix
appatic c' lubul ti tuntah; Caatocoon ti lob.*

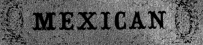

MEXICAN

AMERICAN LANGUAGE.

Totatzin e, ynilhuicac timoyeztica,
Mayectenehualo inmotocatzin.
Mahualauh inmotlatocayotzin.
Machihualo intlalticpac inmotlanequilitzin inyuh chihualo inilhuicac.
Intotlaxcalmomoztla e totechmonequi
maaxcan xitechmomaquili. Maxitechmotlapopolhuili intotlalacol iniuh tiquintlapopolhuia
intechtlatlacalhuia. Macamo xitechmomacahuili inicamo ipan tihuetzizque in teneyecoltiliztli; sanye xitechmomaquixtili inhpuicpa in
amoqualli.

Maiuhmochihua,

MEXICAN.

AMERICAN LANGUAGE.

Totatzin e, ynilhuicac timoyeztica,
Father our heaven in thou art,

Mayectenehualo inmotocatzin;
be hallowed thy name;

Mahualauh inmotlatocayotzin;
may come thy kingdom;

Machihualo intlalticpac inmotlanequilitzin inyuh
be done earth on thy will as

chihualo inilhuicac;
done he is heaven in;

Intotlaxcalmomoztla e totechmonequi maaxcan
bread daily for every one needed useful

xitechmomaquili;
thou us give;

Maxitechmotlapopolhuili intotlalacol iniuh
mayest thou us forgive our debts as

tiquintlapopolhuia intechtlatlacalhuia;
we them forgive us they offend;

Macamo xitechmomacahuili inicamo ipan
that not thou us let that not over

tihuetzizque in teneyecoltiliztli;
we fall temptation;

Canye xitechmomaquixtili inyhuicpa in amoqualli,
but thou us deliver against from not good,

Maiuhmochihua.
May it be done.

ARMENIAN.

ARYAN FAMILY.
SOUTHERN DIVISION.

Dead Language: Old Armenian.— Class: Iranic.

Smyrna 1818.   *Left to Right.*

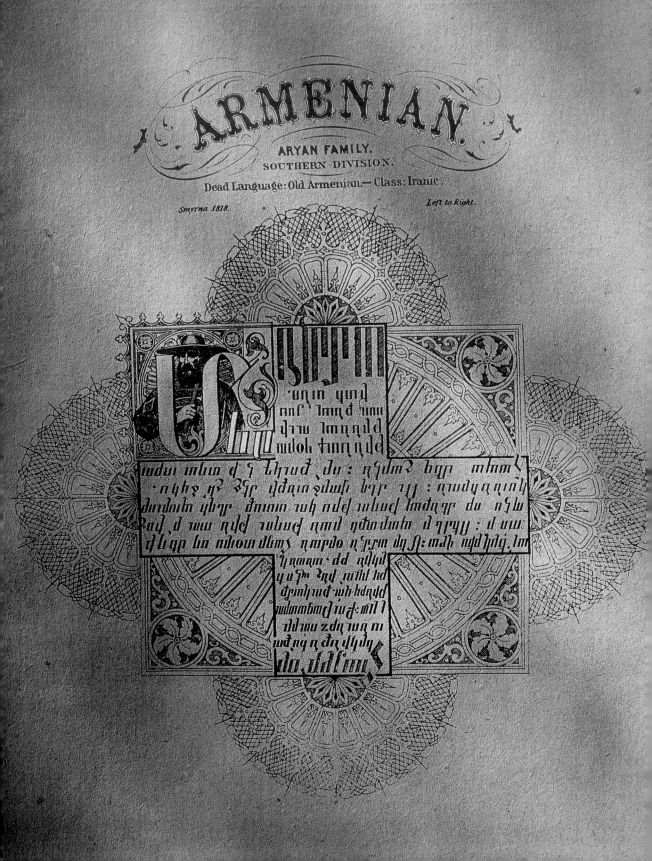

POLISH

ARYAN FAMILY, NORTHERN DIVISION.
DIALECT OF POLAND. BRANCH, WEST SLAVONIC. CLASS, WINDIC.
ST. PETERSBURG, 1815.

Ojcze nasz, któryś jest w niebiosioch, Święć się imię twoje. Przyjdź królewstwo twoje. Bądź wola twoja jako w niebie tak i na ziemli. Ohleba naszega powszedniego dai nam dzisiaj. I odpuść nam nasze winy, jako i my odpuszczamy naszym winowajcóm. I nie wodź nas na pokuszenie; Ale nas zbaw ode zlego.

AMEN.

POLISH.

Ojcze nasz, którys jest w niebiosioch,
Father our, who art in heaven,

Swięć się imię twoje;
hallowed be name thine;

Przyjdz królewstwo twoje;
come kingdom thine;

Bądź wola twoja jako w niebie tak i na ziemli;
be will thine as in heaven also so on earth;

Chleba naszega powszedniego dai nam dzisiaj;
bread ours of every day give us to-day;

I odpuść nam nasze winy, jako i my odpuszczamy
and forgive us our sins, also as we forgive

naszym winowajcóm;
our debtors;

I niewodź nas na pokuszenie;
and not lead us in temptation;

Ale nas zbau ode zlego.
but us deliver from evil.

Amen.
Amen.

DUTCH

ARYAN FAMILY, NORTHERN DIVISION.
DEAD LANGUAGE, OLD DUTCH. BRANCH, LOW GERMAN. CLASS, TEUTONIC.
BERMONDSEY, 1814.

Onze Vader, die in den hemel zijt: uw naam worde geheiligd. Uw koningrijk kome. Uw wil geschiede, gelijk in den hemel alzoo ook op de aarde. Geef ons heden ons dagelijksh brood. En vergeef ons onze shulden, gelijk ook wij vergeven onzen shuldenaren. En leid ons niet in verzocking; maar verlos ons van den booze. Want U. is het koningrijk, en de kracht, en de heerlijkheid tot in alle eeuwigheid.

Amen

Ancient Greek.

(Ἡ Δέησις τοῦ Κυρίου.)

LONDON, 1830.

Π ΑΤΕΡ ἡμῶν ὁ ἐν τοῖς οὐρανοῖς, ἁγιασθήτω
τὸ ὄνομά σου· Ἐλθέτω ἡ βασιλεία
σου· Γενηθήτω τὸ θέλημά σου, ὡς ἐν
οὐρανῷ, καὶ ἐπὶ τῆς γῆς· Τὸν ἄρτον
ἡμῶν τὸν ἐπιούσιον δὸς ἡμῖν σήμερον·
Καὶ ἄφες ἡμῖν τὰ ὀφειλήματα ἡμῶν,
ὡς καὶ ἡμεῖς ἀφίεμεν τοῖς ὀφειλέταις
ἡμῶν· Καὶ μὴ εἰσενέγκῃς ἡμᾶς εἰς πει-
ρασμὸν, ἀλλὰ ῥῦσαι ἡμᾶς ἀπὸ τοῦ
πονηροῦ· Ὅτι σοῦ ἐστιν ἡ βασιλεία, καὶ
ἡ δύναμις, καὶ ἡ δόξα εἰς τοὺς αἰῶνας·

Ἀμήν·

ARABIC

SEMITIC FAMILY.

SOUTHERN DIVISION.

Dialects of Arabic, Amharic, Ethiopic, Himyaritic Inscriptions.

Right to Left   Calcutta 1816.

ابانا نجي
في السموات
يتقدس
ياملكوتك
كا يست و
هيب اد الا
جيب اليها
خبز
ابانا الادلا
كف حنا
ال ال
ان ابا
بلاجيب

GREEK.

DIALECT OF THE DIOCESE OF THESSALIA.

Pater himo, ho an tos oranos,

Agiastita ton onomaso;

Eltheta hi basiliaso;

Genithita ton thelimaso hos an orano ke eptes ges;

Ton arton himon ton epision dos hemon simeron;

Ke aphes himin ta opilimata himon hos ke himes
    aphiemam tis opheleres himon;

Ke mi iselenkis himas is pirasmon;

Alli rhisa himas apo to poniru.

Amin.

ITALIAN

ARYAN FAMILY, NORTHERN DIVISION.
CLASS, ITALIC.
DIODATI, BASLE, 1822.

ATER NOSTRO, che sei ne' cieli, sia santificato il tuo nome. Il tuo regno venga: la tua voluntà sia fatta, siccome in cielo, così anche in terra. Dacci oggi il nostro pane quotidiano. E rimèttici i nostri debiti, siccome noi ancora gli rimèttiamo a' nostri debitori. E non indurci in tentazione: ma liberaci dal maligno. Percicchè tuo è il regno, e la potenza e la gloria in sempiterno.

AMEN.

PURE VENETIAN.

Pare nostro, che si nel Zielo,
Father our, who art in heaven,

Sia santificà el Nome tuo;
be hallowed the name thine;

Vegna el Regno tuo;
come the kingdom thine;

Sia fatta la Volontà tua, siccome in Zielo, così in
be done the will thine, as in heaven, so on

Terra;
earth;

El Pane nostro quotidiano dene ozi;
the bread ours daily give us;

E rimetti a nu i nostri Debiti, siccome nu li
and relieve of us the our debts, as we the

rimettemo ai nostri Debitori;
relieve those our debtors;

E non ne induci in Tentazione;
and not us lead in temptation;

Ma liberene dal Male.
but deliver from evil.

ARABIC.

From the Arabic Bible of the Propaganda:- Rome, 1671.

Abùnà 'llazi fì s-samauâti,
Father our who in the heaven,

Lejatakaddas ismuka ;
hallowed be thy name ;

Letati malkùtuka ;
it come thy kingdom ;

Letakon maschijjatuka fì-kamâ s-samà-i ua 'alal-
it be done will thy in as is heaven the also on

ardì ;
the earth ;

Chobzanà kefàfanà a'tinà l-jauma ;
Our bread that us needful us give to-day ;

Uaghfer lanà kama naghferu uahnu leman achtà-a
forgive and us as forgive we to those debtors

elainà chatâjànà ;
us debts ;

Ua la fì-tod-chelnà t-tagàribi ;
not and lead us in temptation ;

Laken nagginà min asch-scharìrì.
but deliver us from from the evil.

Âmìn.
Amen.

11662.

MOORISH

Syedna wa Abana, Rebby, illadzy phi Smavat, Berkat Ysmic. Elhakkem Melkutick. Yakuhnu kama phi Sma, kadalika ala al Ord, ya Taphi, al Omorik. Aattina Chobzna al Yuhm, ya Siedna Rebby. Ghopher lina Dnubhna, kama smahna Almochottyn. Wa lat kubbluna nattsadchullowa al Lawr, Lakin endschinna min al-Scherir. Laenlak al-Hackam, al-Malake, wa al-Koatsa, wa al-Mesched, illa al-Abdsa.

MOORISH.

Syedna wa Abana, Rebby, illadzy phi Smavat,
Sire our   and Father our   Master   who   in   heaven,

Berkat Ysmic;
blessed   name thine;

Elhakkem Melkutick;
the empire   kingdom thine;

Yakuhnu kama phi Sma, kadalika ala al-Ord, ya
it be done   as   in heaven   so   on the earth,   O

Taphi, al Omorik;
Lord,   the command thine;

Aattina Chobzna al Yuhm, ya Siedna Rebby;
give us   bite our   this day,   O Sire   our Master;

Ghopher lina Dnubhna, kama smahna
forgive   us   sins ours   as   we

Almochottyn;
the debtors;

Wa lat kubbluna, nattsadchullowa al Lawr;
and not   bring us to it   that we are led   in temptation;

Lakin endschinna min al-Scherir:
but   save us   from the   evil:

Laenlak al-Hackam, al-Malake, wa al-Koatsa, wa
for thine (is)   the empire,   the kingdom,   and the power,   and

al-Mesched, illa al-Abdsa.
the   glory,   in the eternity.

A MOORISH TOWN

MOORISH WOMAN

WATER SELLER & BLIND MUSICIAN

A MOORISH GENTLEMAN

A MOORISH GENTLEMAN EATING

A MOOR IN WALKING COSTUME

A MOORISH MINSTREL

THE MOORS
LIVING RACES OF MANKIND

ＳＡＭＡＲＩＴＡＮ.

SEMITIC FAMILY.

Class Hebraic. (...)

Right to Left. *Nablus late Shechem 1800.*

[Samaritan script text]

SAMARITAN.

From Chamberlayne's "Oratio Dom." Amsterdam, 1715.

Abinu shebashomayim,
Father our   the heaven in,

Yicadesh shmoch;
hallowed be   name thine;

Toboh malchutoch;
come   kingdom thine;

Yehee rezonoch kahasher bahsomahyim kane gam
be it   will thine   as it is   in heaven the   also   also

bo,ohrez;
in earth;

Lechem chukeihnu ten lonü hayom;
bread   necessarily   give us   to-day;

Uslaj lohnü choboteinü, ka,asher anajnu solchim
and forgive us   sins ours,   as also   we   forgive

lehchotim kenegdehnu;
to sinners   against us;

Ve,al abiehnu lenisyoh;
and not   lead us   in temptation;

Keeim hahthilenu merooh:
but   free us   from evil;

Kililecho hamlochot ve,hagwühro leolam olomim
for thine   kingdom   and power   for world   worlds.

Amen.
Amen.

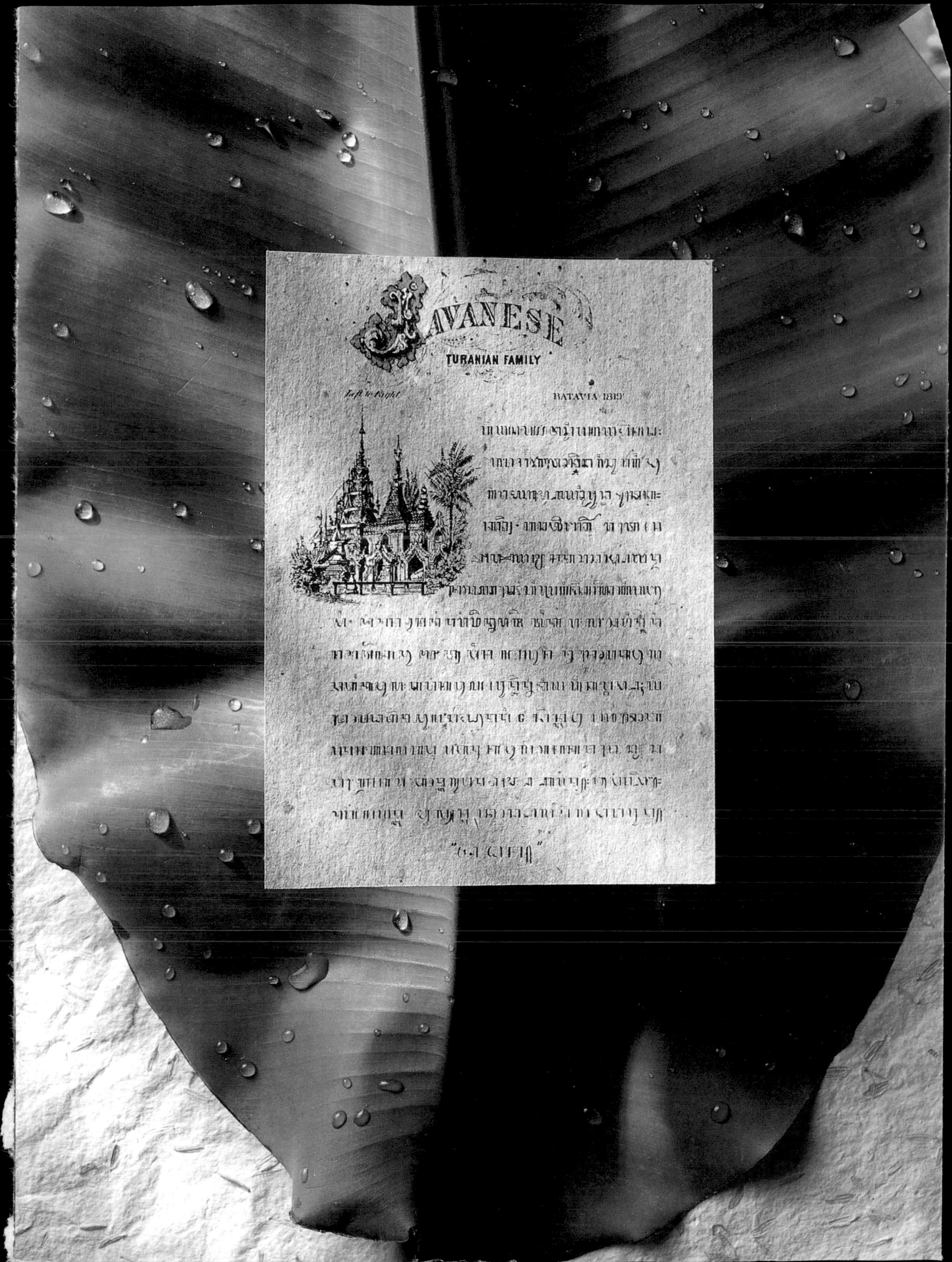
JAVANESE
TURANIAN FAMILY
Left to Right
BATAVIA 1819

JAVANESE.

TURANIAN FAMILY.

From Chamberlayne's Oratio Dom.: Amsterdam, 1715.

Rama kahula kinkan wonten 'in swarga wasta
Father servant (thine) who being in heaven, name

sampêjan dadossa suk'i sag'aman sampêjan
yours be holy, kingdom yours

rawulha karsa sampêjan dadossa 'in bumi kados
come may, will yours be done in earth as

'in swarga reg'ekki kahula kan sadintendinten
in heaven, bread (thy) servant which day by day

sukanni dinten punniki marin kahula 'ambi
give day these to servant (thine); and

puntan marin kahula dôsa kahula kados kahula
pardon on servant debt servant(s) as servant

puntan marin satungiltungil titijan kan salah
forgive on to every one (human) being who sins

marin kahula 'ambi sampun bekta kahula 'in
against servant (thine), and not lead servant in

perk'ôban tapi k'uk'ullaken kahula bari pada
temptation, but make free servant from all

san nawôn sabab sag'aman 'ambi kôwasa sarta
what bad, for kingdom and power with

kamuktên gusti kaguïngannipun dumugi 'in
glory Lord property are till in

nawêt 'amin.
eternity. Amen.

OUR THANKS to the following individuals, libraries and institutions for lending photographs and illustrations:

ENGLISH: "The Golden Rule" by Norman Rockwell, printed by permission of the Norman Rockwell Family Trust. Copyright © 1961 the Norman Rockwell Family Trust.

INTRODUCTION: Photograph of Femme d'Anatolie, 1877, by Abdullah Frères, collection Favod, Musée de l'Elysée, Lausanne, Switzerland.

SPANISH: Torero Julio "Relampaguito" Gomez courtesy of Index Fototeca, Barcelona, Spain. Fabric courtesy of the Board of Trustees of The Victoria & Albert Museum, London.

BURMESE: Postcard photograph of a priest, private collection.

KASHMIR: Vintage postcard, private collection.

BENGAL: Eleventh Bengal Native Cavalry (circa 1890), private collection.

CHEROKEE: "Se-Quo-Yah," Inventor of the Cherokee Alphabet, by C. B. King, neg. no. 319770. Courtesy Department of Library Services, American Museum of Natural History, New York, NY.

FRENCH: Postcard, "Les Petites Roscovites," private collection.

HUNGARIAN: Photograph of peasants, courtesy Hulton Deutsch collection, London.

FINLANDISH: Finnish Workers Band, Warren, Ohio, 1920. Tuomi family photograph, courtesy of The Balch Institute Library, Philadelphia, PA.

GIPSY: Hungarian Gipsies, late nineteenth century, courtesy Hulton Deutsch collection, London.

TURKISH: Turkish Costume, circa 1878, by Firmín Didot et cie, Paris, France. Private collection.

CREDITS

HEBREW: Russian men, Zemil Suttleman family photograph, courtesy of The Balch Institute Library, Philadelphia, PA. Pattern: decoration for the Eastern Wall (mizrah). Podkamien, Poland, 1877. Photograph by John Parnell, courtesy of The Jewish Museum/Art Resource, New York, NY.

WELSH: Women in traditional Welsh dress, Jones family photograph, courtesy of The Balch Institute Library, Philadelphia, PA.

CHINESE: Ruth Tomwye wedding to Felton Chow, 1925, courtesy of The Balch Institute Library, Philadelphia, PA.

GERMAN: Postcard dated 1914, folk costume of Schaumburg-Lippe, private collection.

PERSIAN: Rizzledash Chiefs, courtesy Hulton Deutsch collection, London.

RUSSIAN: Abazinian woman "Loow Aul," neg. no. 337114,

Courtesy the Department of Library Services, American Museum of Natural History, New York, NY.

HOTTENTOT: Copper plate engraving from Modern History, 1733. Beads courtesy of Ignacio Villarreaz at Craft Caravan, New York, NY.

IRISH: Two Connemara girls, courtesy Hulton Deutsch collection, London.

MEXICAN, MAYU: Market scene in San Luis Potosi, private collection. Serape from Paula Rubenstein, Ltd, New York, NY.

ARMENIAN: Cabinet portrait, J.K. Wilking family, courtesy of The Balch Institute Library, Philadelphia, PA.

POLISH: Old postcard of "Krakowiak," the Polish National dance, private collection.

DUTCH: Costume illustration, courtesy of the Argosy Gallery, New York, NY.

GREEK: Athenian woman, courtesy of The Balch Institute Library Atlantis collection, Philadelphia, PA. Fabric courtesy of the Board of Trustees of The Victoria & Albert Museum, London.

ARABIC: Vintage postcard, private collection.

ITALIAN: Capri costume, sepia photograph, private collection.

MOORISH: Early British postcard, private collection.

SAMARITAN: Postcard, Samaritan high priest and scroll, Jerusalem, private collection.

JAVANESE: Photograph of Javanese dancer by Francis S. Woodbury, collection Favod, Musée de l'Elysée, Lausanne, Switzerland. Fabric courtesy of the Board of Trustees of The Victoria & Albert Museum, London.